WITHDRAWN

True Freedom

TRUE
FREEDOM

OLIVER
NORTH
and BRIAN SMITH

Multnomah® Publishers *Sisters, Oregon*

TRUE FREEDOM
published by Multnomah Publishers, Inc.

© 2004 by Oliver North and Brian Smith
International Standard Book Number: 1-59052-363-6

Cover design by Brand Navigators LLC.
Cover image by Kamil Vojnar/Photonica

Unless otherwise indicated, Scripture quotations are from:
The Holy Bible, New International Version
© 1973, 1984 by International Bible Society,
used by permission of Zondervan Publishing House

Other Scripture quotations are from:
The Holy Bible, King James Version (KJV)

Multnomah is a trademark of Multnomah Publishers, Inc.,
and is registered in the U.S. Patent and Trademark Office.
The colophon is a trademark of Multnomah Publishers, Inc.

For information:
MULTNOMAH PUBLISHERS, INC.
POST OFFICE BOX 1720
SISTERS, OREGON 97759

Library of Congress Cataloging-in-Publication Data

North, Oliver.
    True freedom / by Oliver North and Brian Smith.
        p. cm.
Includes bibliographical references.
    ISBN 1-59052-363-6 (hardcover)
1. Prayer. 2. Liberty—Religious aspects—Christianity. I. Smith, Brian, 1960-
II. Title.

    BV210.3.N67 2004
    248.3'2—dc22

                                                    2003021187

04 05 06 07 08 09 10—10 9 8 7 6 5 4 3 2 1 0

Contents

Chapter One

THE PROVEN PATHWAY TO FREEDOM

Lord, I seek you with all my heart,
with all the strength you have given me.
I long to understand that which I believe.
You created me in order to find you;
you gave me strength to seek you.
My strength and my weakness are in your hands:
preserve my strength, and help my weakness.
Where you have already opened the door, let me come in;
where it is shut, open at my knocking.

AUGUSTINE OF HIPPO (354–430)

There I lay, writhing in the North Carolina sand. I couldn't feel my legs. Piercing pain gripped my back, as though someone had skewered me with a railroad spike. How could this happen...*now* of all times?

I wanted a medic and some quick relief.

But God was about to give me something better. In my pain-fogged panic, I had no way of knowing that my whole life would turn on this moment.

TUG-OF-WAR WITH GOD

God has protected and blessed me all my life. But for more than thirty years I failed to acknowledge His active, personal interest. Through all those years, He patiently coaxed me toward the pathway to true freedom (I can see that now), but I persisted in blundering down my own path in determined ignorance.

As a child growing up in the Catholic church, I never doubted God's existence, and I learned to respect Him deeply. From a distance.

Years later God showed that He was closer to me than I was willing to admit. My friends and I were driving through heavy snow late at night on a weekend ski trip. It was 1964, my first year at the naval academy. Everyone had fallen asleep…including the driver. I jerked awake just in time to see the headlights of the oncoming truck. Then we hit.

The carnage was terrible. One of my friends was killed, and the other three were badly mangled. In comparison, my injuries were relatively minimal—head injuries, crushed vertebrae in my lower spine, broken nose, broken jaw, broken leg, and one damaged knee. But my surgeries and recovery kept me down for months.

I fought my way back. Sure, I gave God His credit. During my stay at the naval hospital, I made it my daily habit to wheel into the hospital chapel to pray. And God healed me so completely that four years later I won the brigade boxing championship. But my relationship with God was still one-sided—I sent up my requests, and He took care of me. I simply wasn't listening to what He was trying to tell me.

Prayer is like a two-way radio, which is designed both to transmit and receive. But my radio was stuck on "transmit." I thought, more than anything else, that my own dogged persistence had brought me back to health and allowed me to finish my academy training. I was determined to become a marine, and I was sure no obstacle was insurmountable.

God stuck by me through my year in Vietnam, as I patrolled the so-called demilitarized zone. On several occasions, men standing right next to me were killed, while I was either untouched or back in action in very short order.

God also saved me from another kind of disaster. In my zealous commitment to the Marine Corps, I almost threw away two of His greatest gifts to me—my marriage and my family.

In the early 1970s, I found myself doing what I

enjoyed more than anything else—training marines in Okinawa. When I wrote to my wife, Betsy, that I would be missing my second Christmas in a row with her and the kids, she took longer than usual to respond. In her next letter, she wrote, "I've had enough. I want a divorce. Here's the name of my attorney."

I tried to tell myself that I didn't care, that my work was the only truly important priority. But the honest part of me—the part that hurt so desperately—wouldn't buy it. The internal struggle took its toll. I ended up in the hospital, my exhausted body racked with bronchitis and my tormented spirit mired in clinical depression. I reluctantly submitted to psychiatric care and then marriage counseling, gradually recovering and ultimately reconciling with Betsy. But even through those excruciating days, I still imagined that my progress and my healing were the results of my own hard work.

One early promotion followed another, only because I was a good officer. Or so I thought.

All the while, God was preparing my wake-up call.

DIVINE INTRUSION

By 1978, I had known Lieutenant Colonel John Grinalds for about three years. He was on the fast track through the ranks. Top of his class at West Point and highly decorated from his two tours of duty in Vietnam, he had gone on to become a Rhodes Scholar and White House Fellow and to earn a Harvard MBA.

Oh, and there was one other characteristic that set Grinalds apart from the rest. He was one of those "born-again Christians." Whatever that meant. Along with all the usual training and administrative manuals on his desk, he kept a Bible. Right there in plain sight. And he *read* it.

Grinalds was assigned as a battalion commander to the Second Marine Division, based at Camp Lejeune, and he honored me by asking me to come along as his operations officer. I was happy to hitch my wagon to his rapidly rising star. In my new role, I was third in command, responsible for the training and preparation of a two-thousand-man unit for deployment to the Mediterranean.

One morning, about two weeks before we were due to deploy, our battalion was conducting a training exercise. I had just adjusted the antenna on an armored amphibious vehicle and, spurning the ladder on the side, jumped to the ground.

Big mistake.

Instant memories of the 1964 car accident flashed through my pain-racked mind. I had reinjured my back in exactly the same place. Aside from the wish for unconsciousness, my one overriding thought was, *I just blew my chance to deploy with these men.* I knew from having experienced a similar reinjury in a 1973 parachute accident that I was due for at least two weeks of hospitalization and bed rest.

I lay writhing on the ground. Couldn't feel my legs. Lost control of my bladder.

Before a medic could arrive, John Grinalds showed up. Next thing I knew, he was putting his hands on my legs and saying, "I'm going to pray for you."

Pray? I thought. *I'm lying here in agony, and you want to pray!*

But what I said aloud was, "Uh, Colonel, don't you think we could just do this the usual way? You know, get the helicopter, go to the hospital…?"

But Grinalds ignored me. He called out, "Lord Jesus Christ, You are the Great Physician. Heal this man."

In that very instant the pain disappeared. Soon the feeling returned to my legs. When I was ready, Grinalds helped me to my feet.

Astonished, I came out with one of the most inane utterances of my life. I said, "Thank you, sir."

At that, Grinalds grabbed me by my jacket and pulled me up to his face. "Don't thank me," he said. "Thank your Lord and Savior. *He* is the Great Physician. You have to turn to *Him.*"

EMBARKING INTO FREEDOM

That incident was the two-by-four God used to break through my thick-skulled resistance. I had it in my head that freedom meant taking care of myself, forging my own path through the jungle of life's challenges. I knew that God was there to help, but I expected Him to follow my lead. What I came to realize was that He had been leading all along—and that I had not done well at following. I had been placing my faith in myself, yet He had been telling me over and over, "You'll only be truly free when you know and trust Me."

This realization profoundly humbled me. During the six months of our Mediterranean deployment, I participated in Bible studies with Grinalds and managed to read the Bible cover to cover. I learned that I had known a lot *about* God, but I had not *known Him* personally. I had sent a lot of orders in His direction, and He had even deigned to "obey" some of them. But I had been living in servitude to self; now I was discovering true freedom, living as I was designed to live—in relationship with God.

I had grown up believing in the vending machine concept of prayer—you put in your quarter, and you get back your selection, all neatly wrapped and sealed. But now I've come to understand that prayer is freely flowing, two-way conversation with a Person. In fact, prayer doesn't even require words.

When I'm consciously *with God,* that's prayer.

When I look to Him with an attitude of dependence, that's prayer.

Prayer at its best involves intimate, heart-to-heart communion with God, with or without words.

My friend Jarod came to this realization the day he slammed his thumb in his car door. The door was locked, his right thumb was stuck—sending frantic pain signals to his brain—and his car keys were in his right pocket. As he gingerly reached across his body with his left hand, digging for his keys, his whispered plea was simply, "Lord." Both he and God knew exactly what he needed at that moment. More words were superfluous.

John Bunyan, seventeenth-century author of *Pilgrim's Progress,* wrote, "The best prayers have often more groans than words."

FAITH AND TRUE FREEDOM

Closely related to prayer is the concept of faith—a concept that is widely misunderstood. Some people think faith is a power we somehow stir up within ourselves, and when we somehow muster enough of it (however much "enough" is), God responds and answers our prayers. But according to the Bible, faith is an attitude that acknowledges my utter powerlessness—my need to depend on

God (see John 15:5; 2 Corinthians 12:9).

Prayer is the voice of faith…and the pathway to true freedom.

But that won't make much sense unless we understand freedom, which can be conceived in a variety of ways. There's the physical freedom that comes with a healthy body and independent movement. There's political freedom, which has always meant so much to me. But we in the United States of America enjoy political freedom only because our nation's founders had appropriated something even more basic, which for the purpose of this book we will call *true freedom*.

True freedom is the opposite of arrogant self-determination. It is submission to God's will. When I enthrone my own will and pursue my own "best," I severely limit myself. When I obey God, I open myself to His unlimited blessing. Jesus Himself said that if you obey His teachings, then "you will know the truth, and the truth will set you free" (John 8:32).

How can you learn to trust God enough to submit yourself to His will? Only by growing to know Him. Only by living life in conversation with Him. Only through a lifestyle of prayer. Your Creator and Lord wants to relate to you as Friend and Father. He made you for one primary purpose—to live in intimate relationship with Him. When you fulfill that purpose, you find true freedom.

Prayer makes a difference *inside us*—through prayer

our hearts and minds become attuned to God's heart and mind, and we begin to think what He thinks and desire what He desires.

It's been said that if you've only seen an eagle in a cage, you've never seen an eagle. An eagle was meant for the wide skies and the cold winds of the heights. Just as the eagle was meant to cast himself freely upon the wind, so we were meant to cast ourselves on God, the Mighty One whose hand unrolled those skies like a parchment. We were not designed to be enslaved to self, but to soar freely according to His purpose and design.

We are God's, and only He can sustain our flight.

PRAYER PRINCIPLE #1:

Prayer liberates us to live as we were designed,
in intimate relationship with God.

Chapter Two

FREE FROM
THE PAST

PRAYER AND MY GUILT

O my Lord, since it seems you are determined to save me,
I ask that you may do so quickly.
And since you have decided to dwell within me,
I ask that you clean your house,
wiping away all the grime of sin.
TERESA OF AVILA (1515–1582)

I had more housecleaning to do than I realized.

During the years following my reconciliation with
Betsy, I corrected my pattern of negligence. I became
more attentive to her and the kids, spending as much time
at home with them as possible. My work was still important, and I was gone for months at a time, but Betsy and
I now related as loving partners—not as commander and
subordinate.

Nonetheless, I felt guilty for all the lost time. Had I somehow damaged my children by my neglect during the formative stages? Had I so wounded Betsy's trust at some level that I could never regain it? There was no way I could erase the pain of abandonment they had suffered as so many birthdays and Christmases had passed with my chair sitting empty. Could I make up the lost ground?

And even if all these practical issues could be rectified, my conscience told me that I had done wrong, pure and simple. Could I ever find peace? Or would the guilt plague me for the rest of my life?

It wasn't until that crisis point in 1978, when I made a new beginning in my relationship with God, that I found the answers. As I drew close to God and came to understand how He viewed me, He liberated me from my past through forgiveness.

I was familiar with the Catholic confessional. But an entirely new world opened up to me when I began to know God personally. As a son, I grew to see my Father's heart of love and compassion. In this atmosphere of acceptance, my confessions of guilt—now conveyed directly to Him, not through a human priest—gave me a new depth of peace and freedom. I didn't have to guess whether I was forgiven…I *knew*.

Two Approaches to Guilt

In our culture, people have a strong tendency to avoid responsibility for personal guilt. Contemporary psychology wants to minimize sin and to convince us that we're only dealing with guilt *feelings*—not real guilt. If you can learn to think and feel differently about your past, we're told, then you can discover release and fulfillment. No need to say you actually did anything wrong. That will only harm your self-esteem. Forgive yourself, and move on.

I know there is such a thing as misplaced or false guilt. We all experience guilt feelings over actions that aren't really wrong. In fact, false guilt is one of Satan's most useful tools, by which he can totally paralyze a person.

There is also, however, such a thing as very *real* guilt in all of us. (Please stay with me while we navigate the bad news, because good news is coming!) Romans 6:23 *doesn't* say, "For the wages of guilt feelings is anxiety." It says, "For the wages of sin is death."

I've stood as the defendant in a courtroom, and I've experienced the gut-wrenching grief of hearing my name attached to a guilty verdict. In 1988 a federal grand jury indicted me on sixteen criminal charges—later reduced to twelve—for alleged misconduct during my service with the National Security Council. A year later, at the end of my trial, the judge read the trial jury's verdict, and three times I heard that damning word: "Guilty."

I never want to hear that again. Though subsequent appeal would completely exonerate me, I had no way of knowing that as the judge's words pummeled me. My heart sank through the courthouse floor.

But my earthly experience is nothing compared to the courtroom scene in heaven, with God the Judge on His bench issuing an eternal death sentence for my sin. No appeal in all the universe could remove the fact that I deserve that sentence.

Fortunately, the scene in heaven doesn't end there. Romans 6:23 continues, "But the gift of God is eternal life in Christ Jesus our Lord." As seriously as we must take the reality of our guilt, even more astounding is the complete extent of God's forgiveness.

We receive the forgiveness God offers by asking for it. By praying.

The world tries to deal with guilt feelings by changing the way we think or feel. When we pray, God deals with our real guilt by creating us anew through the Cross of Christ. Because Jesus died in our place, taking the eternal punishment we deserve, God is able to declare us "not guilty," opening the way for us to be restored to right relationship with Him.

The apostle Paul knew this as well as anyone who has lived. Before he became Paul the apostle, he was Saul the Pharisee, the guardian of the Jewish faith. In his zealous ignorance, he saw Christians as heretics, and he hunted down and sent to prison and death many of God's dearly loved children. If anyone's history should have haunted him, it was Saul's.

But after he learned that he had been persecuting the very God he thought he was serving (Acts 9:4–5), Saul was overwhelmed to find that God's freedom extended even to him. In 1 Timothy 1:16 he later explained, "But...I was shown mercy so that in me, the worst of sinners, Christ Jesus might display his unlimited patience as an example for those who would believe on him and receive eternal life."

If God could free Saul, "the worst of sinners," from his guilt, then God's forgiveness is adequate to cover your past as well.

NEW FREEDOM EACH DAY

Freedom from guilt is a renewable resource.

Even after salvation, as God's children, we continue to confess to Him the ways we've offended Him—not because our salvation is in any danger, but to prevent anything from hindering our intimacy with Him. Most literally, 1 John 1:9 says, "If we *keep on confessing* our sins, he is faithful and just and will *keep on forgiving* us our sins" (my paraphrase). Confession should be a part of our ongoing conversation with God, as often as we need it.

God is not motivated by some morbid desire to make us feel worse. We already feel bad, and He offers us freedom, peace, and joy. Coming clean with God is liberating because His forgiveness frees us from both the penalty of our sin and the feelings of remorse that go with it.

Aaron and Cindy found this freedom. Pastor Gordon Reeves first met the enthusiastic couple within weeks after they had come to faith in Christ. They marveled at the completeness of God's forgiveness, available simply for the asking. They were especially grateful because they knew better than anyone how much sin He had forgiven.

Aaron and Cindy wanted a fresh start, so they prayed that God would show them how they needed to change. They were not married, and one of their first steps was to receive God's forgiveness for their sexual impurity. Then they agreed to live separately and abstinently throughout the four months leading up to their wedding.

During their first year of marriage, as they prayed for further direction, phantoms from their past crept in and threatened their sense of freedom. Each of them had stolen clothes, purses, wallets—anything that might get them a few fast dollars. They had used cocaine and, even worse, had dealt a little of it to other people, including some teens.

At times they wondered if God could possibly accept them, but Gordon encouraged them to keep pursuing God through prayer and His Word.

The road was rough. Cindy experienced several months of depression, and she and Aaron had to separate for a few weeks. But they kept seeking God, learning about His gracious heart. One by one, the phantoms were disbursed by God's forgiveness. The wounds found His healing.

Over the years, Aaron's and Cindy's freedom and increasing maturity opened the door for them to impact other lives through small-group leadership. They even became involved in training other leaders to shepherd people toward freedom.

Purifying Freedom

How about you? Do you carry your past guilt around with you? Do you wish you could find the peace that the world can't offer or understand? Because Jesus died for you, you can come directly into the presence of the Judge of the universe and call Him "Father" (1 Peter 1:17). Awesome thought!

None of us is worthy of forgiveness, but God experiences genuine delight when we accept it. Go ahead and talk to Him. Freedom is yours for the asking.

Prayer Principle #2:

Prayer brings continually renewed freedom from guilt.

Chapter Three

FREE IN THE PRESENT

PRAYER AND SIN'S POWER

Rule over me this day, O God,
leading me on the path of righteousness.
Put your Word in my mind and your Truth in my heart,
that this day I neither think nor feel anything except what is
good and honest. Protect me from all lies and falsehood,
helping me to discern deception wherever I meet it.
Let my eyes always look straight ahead on the road you wish
me to tread, that I might not be tempted by any distraction.
And make my eyes pure, that no false desires
may be awakened within me.

JACOB BOEHME (1575–1624)

Walt was devastated. He had worked twenty-eight faithful
years as a sales representative for Michael, a small business
owner and fellow Christian. After nearly three decades of

loyalty and friendship, the pain of betrayal was overwhelming. A chill settled over his heart, and he began to wonder if he could ever trust anyone again.

Maybe this is payback for the people I cheated, Walt thought. But that had been so long ago. He and his accountability buddies had prayed, and God had changed Walt's heart.

In fact, it was because of Walt's strengthened conviction that he was so alarmed to catch Michael, his employer, justifying dishonesty with customers. Awkwardly, Walt confronted Michael, wanting to express brotherly concern.

At first Michael made excuses. "You have no idea how hard it is to keep this business afloat in today's economy. And if the customer doesn't know he's paying extra, why should I worry?"

"You're not just hurting them," Walt said. "You're hurting yourself, and you're offending God."

"Okay," Michael finally agreed. "You're right. I'll be more careful."

Michael was careful for a week. When Walt discovered him padding estimates and invoices, Walt expressed his concern again. This time Michael said nothing.

A few days later Michael fired Walt. "You've just become too hard to work with," he said. "You're not a team player."

Suddenly, after twenty-eight years, Walt was unemployed.

Walt struggled with depression for over a year. He spent the first five months finding his next, lower paying, job. He felt guilty for providing less for his family, and he snapped irritably at them for the slightest reason.

Walt wrestled daily with bitterness. He refused to forgive Michael, and he avoided talking to God. But when the burden became too heavy, he finally cried out, "God, take it away!"

Broken, Walt asked a few Christian friends to pray for spiritual victory. Nothing changed on the outside. Same job, same family, same broken friendship. But inside, Walt began to heal and strengthen.

He later heard that Michael had lost his business. The day Walt anonymously contributed fifty dollars to a fund to support Michael and his family was the day Walt knew God had granted him true freedom.

ASKING FOR GRACE

Because the daily battle against the power of sin is far more than you or I can handle alone, we who wish to live in freedom have no choice but to cast ourselves upon God for the grace to live clean, upright lives in the present.

Paul wrote to the young pastor Titus, "For the grace of God that brings salvation has appeared to all men. It teaches us to say 'No' to ungodliness and worldly passions, and to live self-controlled, upright and godly lives in this present age" (Titus 2:11–12).

Did you notice which supernatural force Paul identified as the power for godly living? It wasn't God's truth, holiness, or justice. Paul said that it is God's *grace* that teaches us to deny the power of sin in our daily lives.

God's grace basically means He showers us with favor we don't deserve. By grace He unconditionally forgives the humble sinner, and by grace He empowers us to do freely what we were made to do—to live a holy life.

In the preceding chapter we looked at 1 John 1:9, but we didn't finish examining the verse. When we confess our sins, not only does God forgive us our sins, but He is also "faithful and just…to purify us from all unrighteousness." When we come to God humbly, honestly, and frequently, He cleans house, removing unrighteousness and replacing it with the righteous character of Jesus Christ so that we are better able to stand our moral ground in the ongoing spiritual battle.

WE'RE NOT ISLANDS

Through prayer we not only liberate *ourselves* for holy living—we can also help *others* conquer sin's power. Jan's heart broke as she watched her son Jason go his own destructive way, first through high school, then as a young adult. She knew he was sleeping with his girlfriend and drinking too much. His nightly partying had gotten Jason into numerous scrapes with the law, and Jan feared for his safety. Even for his life.

Jan's lectures to Jason had little effect. She felt utterly helpless, so she began to petition the Lord on her son's behalf. She reasoned that if God can turn a king's heart like a river (Proverbs 21:1), He might change her son's heart.

Over the years, time and again, God demonstrated His sovereignty over Jason's mind and conscience. On one occasion Jan knew that Jason was on his way to a no-holds-barred party, and she prayed he would be stopped. The next day she learned that on his way to the party he had simply changed his mind and gone to sit by a river and think.

Today Jason—still a young man—shows signs of giving up his resistance to God. He broke off his unhealthy relationship with his girlfriend and has cultivated an honest openness with his mom.

Jan's persistent pursuit of her Lord is bearing fruit of eternal value in her son's life.

POWER ON ALL FRONTS

Prayer opens a variety of avenues leading to God's liberating grace. For example, time in God's presence can free us from the cycle of defeat due to "trapped" or obsessive thinking. He helps us overcome the obsessive desire for control, the relentless sense of inadequacy, or the emotional addiction to a sinful habit.

In response to prayer, God can overcome modern idolatry—the devotion of our hearts to anything in His place. As we grow to know God's heart, He naturally assumes His rightful place as Lord in our lives.

Prayer also leads to freedom from the power of outright spiritual attack. Shel Arensen, a missionary in Kenya, tells of what started out as a typical Sunday worship service in Kijabe. In the middle of the service, Shel noticed a disruption. A woman, dressed only in a petticoat, squeezed her way into a crowded row and began to chew on the wooden benches.

She was escorted from the service, but over the following days, as they observed her strange behavior, Shel and several others became convinced that she was demon-possessed. They learned that her name was Rose, and they felt compelled to pray for her liberation. She was admitted to the hospital, and the believers prayed in her presence and in sessions elsewhere on a daily basis, for hours at a time. Some of them fasted on her behalf. After a couple of days, Rose received Christ as her Savior, but she was still deeply troubled.

As they talked with Rose, the missionaries learned that she had been terribly hurt by her father and that her bitterness had become a stronghold for the demons. They encouraged her to forgive her father. At first she refused, but after several days she said, "I'm ready. I forgive him."

From that point on, the praying believers were able to free Rose from the powerful influence of several demons, and she has since continued to grow and heal in the Lord.

It's a fitting epilogue to note that after Rose met with her father and forgave him in person, he was so impressed that he also asked to become a Christian. Indirectly, the prayers of these faithful people allowed him also to experience the freedom Rose had discovered.[1]

POWER FOR THE PRESENT

Think about the battles you fight each day. Are you fighting on your own…and losing? Or winning for now, believing you have things under control? Or have you sought the face of God your Father for His powerfully liberating grace?

In response to prayer, God solidifies our true freedom from the stranglehold of sin. We can be certain, through prayer, that we're now alive to a new destiny over which sin no longer holds power (Romans 6:6–8, 17–18). By the Spirit we're enabled to move beyond our old self and to press forward into a life as new as tomorrow's sunrise.

Whatever power sin might exercise in your life, God has promised He will always provide a way of escape (1 Corinthians 10:13). He'll lead you to it if you'll stay close by Him.

PRAYER PRINCIPLE #3:

Prayer frees us from the stranglehold of sin's power.

Chapter Four

FREE FOR THE FUTURE

PRAYER AND MY FEAR

Do with me as is best for you,
For that will be best for me too.
Whether I live or die, I am with you,
And you are with me.
Lord, I wait for your salvation
And for your kingdom.

DIETRICH BONHOEFFER (1906–1945)

Few Christians in the history of the world have faced the future with such courage and freedom as did Dietrich Bonhoeffer.

Bonhoeffer was a German Lutheran minister who actively opposed the 1930s Nazi movement. He foresaw the brutality that would arise from this godless philosophy.

When World War II broke out, he attempted to unite the efforts of anti-Nazi Germans and the British government. At one point he escaped Germany with his life, but later he returned to his home country in an effort to rally German resistance. In 1943 he was imprisoned for conspiring to assassinate Hitler. It was two years later, upon hearing that he had been sentenced to be hanged, that Bonhoeffer expressed to God the words of hope and emotional honesty that opened this chapter.

Very few of us will ever have to deal with the anxiety that accompanies a looming execution, but in the face of our own smaller anxieties, God offers the same kind of hope and bedrock peace that Bonhoeffer expressed as he anticipated his death. Bonhoeffer didn't achieve this amazing perspective merely by being a good man. He found it in the presence of the God who controls the future.

Think about the fears and worries that frequently—maybe constantly—haunt you as you look ahead. At their very root, our anxieties reflect our doubts that God is powerful enough, smart enough, or caring enough to act in our best interest.

It's only as we spend time in God's presence and in His Word that we can experience His faithfulness firsthand. There we come face-to-face with the God who proves Himself to be *almighty* (powerful enough), *all wise* (smart enough) and *unconditionally loving* (caring enough). In His presence we find freedom from our anxiety about the future. He'll take care of us.

KNOWING THE ONE WE CAN TRUST

Facing his own execution in a lonely dungeon, the apostle Paul drew upon decades of intimate, personal knowledge of God and wrote, "I know whom I have believed, and am convinced that he is able to guard what I have entrusted to him for that day" (2 Timothy 1:12). In other words, "I know God so well that there isn't the slightest doubt in my mind that He will take care of me—right up until the end of my life, and beyond."

My family and I were challenged with this lesson many times during one of the most trying episodes of my life. During the mid-1980s, under the direction of the National Security Council and the president, I was involved simultaneously in two covert and politically explosive operations—one to rescue American hostages by selling arms to Iran, and the other to provide material support to the Nicaraguan contras, who were trying to overthrow Daniel Ortega's brutal Sandinista dictatorship.

When I recognized that both operations were about to become public knowledge, I was prepared to be the political scapegoat. But in November 1986, when I was fired on national TV by the president, the attorney general mentioned that my activity might involve "criminality."

The comment floored me. I was suddenly facing the possibility of criminal charges for actions that had *never* been criminally motivated. Indeed, over a year later, after enduring grueling, drawn-out congressional hearings, I found myself a defendant in federal court, confronting a list of twelve counts.

Please understand, my purpose in sharing this story here is not to defend myself. I've already explained all the details elsewhere. I don't want the question of my guilt or innocence to distract from my real point—to show how God, in response to prayer, sustained my family in the face of a traumatically uncertain future. For a matter of years my family did not know whether I would be taken from them and imprisoned. Neither did I.

LEARNING TO WAIT

Because God had demonstrated His faithfulness to me earlier in my life, as I described in chapter 1, I already knew that I would not be facing this ordeal alone. But God gave me another reminder. On my first day of testimony before Congress, an elderly lady I'd never seen before slipped through security and handed me a small card.

At first my protective attorney, Brendan Sullivan, confiscated it, but after we sat in our places, he read the card and then propped it against the microphone on the table in front of me. He developed a routine over the several days of my testimony—every time we left, he put the card in his pocket. Then when we returned, he put the card back in front of me.

The truth printed on that card helped sustain me through that experience and the years to come, and I still carry it with me to this day. The card reads:

> They that wait upon the LORD shall renew their strength; they shall mount up with wings as eagles; they shall run, and not be weary; and they shall walk, and not faint.
>
> ISAIAH 40:31, KJV

Throughout those five long years, my family and I were publicly smeared and became the subject of wild rumors and fanciful news stories—even a TV miniseries that was produced and aired without a minute's consultation with us. The pressure was such that without the Lord, I'm confident Betsy and I would have parted ways, and my four children could have become disillusioned and cynical. I can't say that we were free from anxiety and fear. But I can say that God answered prayer by sustaining our confidence in His sovereign control and ultimate victory in our lives.

Betsy and I, our pastors, and members of our small Bible study group prayed unceasingly. And we received literally millions of letters from people across the nation, many of whom promised their prayers. (In fact, if you were one of those, please accept my thanks for helping preserve our sanity, our integrity, and our good name.)

In the end, after first receiving a guilty verdict on three counts, I was completely exonerated upon appeal. But the greater victory was that we held on to God through the worst, knowing all along that He was hanging on to us.

LET GOD DO HIS JOB

When we pray about our fears, we place the outworking of our future where it belongs—in the hands of God. Peter, Jesus' good friend, who had often tried to solve his problems in his own way, learned this lesson well: "Cast all your anxiety on him, because he cares for you" (1 Peter 5:7).

When Sandra's daughter Jamie entered school, Sandra joined the PTA, volunteered in Jamie's class, and by all possible means positioned herself to watch over Jamie and her teachers to ensure that everything went well. She made sure Jamie picked up materials she might otherwise have forgotten. She stepped in when she thought Jamie had been misunderstood. She was compelled by an urgency to fix or prevent any problems that might arise for Jamie, and she worried constantly.

Then she learned of Moms in Touch International, a ministry that coordinates mothers into groups that pray for their children and the school. As she began praying faithfully for Jamie, Sandra found herself released from her anxiety over her daughter. She realized she had been taking on a task that only God could fulfill.

Sandra saw God answer countless prayers for Jamie and the children of other moms with whom she prayed. She prayed for God to give Jamie's teachers wisdom. In response, God created several close and valuable teacher-student relationships for Jamie. As Jamie grew older, sometimes Sandra would pray that if her daughter did something seriously wrong she would be caught…and she was. After a few such episodes, Jamie realized that she couldn't get away with troublemaking, and her behavior noticeably improved.

Sandra learned that parenting is, in part, a process of transferring her children to a new Parent, who will watch over them throughout the rest of their lives. She could trust God to do His job.

FACING THE UNKNOWN

God often challenges us to grow in faith by making us wait for His answer, sometimes for years or decades. We keep ourselves free from anxiety during the dry spells through persistent prayer, continually affirming to God that He is faithful and sovereign (Luke 11:5–10; 18:1–8).

In prayer, we also acknowledge to God our freedom

from needing all the answers. When God allows mystery in our lives, we can learn to trust Him with the unknown by drawing closer to His heart.

And if nothing else makes sense, the Bible leaves no doubt that whatever may happen between now and the final chapter of our life story, we who are in Christ are guaranteed the ultimate happy ending (Revelation 21–22).

Following my initial conviction on three criminal counts, before my appeal cleared my name, I had to be sentenced for my conviction. On sentencing day I had spent extra time with the Lord, and as I walked to the courtroom, one of the ever-present reporters said to me, "You look awfully calm for a man on his way in to be sentenced."

"That's because I know where I'm going," I replied.

He looked astonished. "You do? How many years are you going to get?"

"Eternity," I replied.

GIVE YOURSELF A BREAK

Jesus encouraged us, "Do not let your hearts be troubled. Trust in God; trust also in me." And He explained that He was going ahead of us to prepare our home in heaven, where we will join Him for eternity (see John 14:1–3). He also invited us, "Come to me…and I will give you rest" (Matthew 11:28).

When was the last time you enjoyed the rest that is available to you in the presence of the Lord?

PRAYER PRINCIPLE #4:

Prayer frees us from anxiety as we come to know God's faithful heart.

Chapter Five

FREE TO KNOW
WHO I AM

Prayer and Self-Deception

O Light everlasting, surpassing all created light!
Pour forth from heaven the glorious rays of your light,
and pierce the dark depths of my soul. Purify, gladden and
enlighten my soul, that it may turn to you in joy.
I know that the shadow of sin still hangs over me.
I know that I fight against your light, preferring the gloom of
worldly pride to the bright sunshine of true humility.
Yet you, who can make the raging sea calm,
can bring peace to my soul. You, who turn night into day,
can bring gladness to my miserable soul.

Thomas à Kempis (c. 1380–1471)

Parents were never meant to outlive their kids.

Rebecca had heard this statement before, but only now
did she comprehend the weight of sorrow it contained. Her

grief over the loss of her sixteen-year-old son Jerry seemed as fresh and raw now, several weeks later, as it had on the day of his funeral.

Rebecca had tried many times to resume her habit of daily prayer and Bible reading, but words just didn't seem to work anymore. She found herself unable to focus on God's Word to her, and she experienced great difficulty formulating prayers.

But even in the midst of her pain, Rebecca remembered one fundamental, unshakable truth: She knew she was God's daughter.

At a loss for words, Rebecca discovered a new way to relate to her Father. She pictured God the Father sitting on His throne in her living room, His great robes flowing around the throne. She imagined herself walking into the room, falling down at His feet, nestling into the folds of His robes, and simply laying her head on His lap. There she rested each day, in His silent comfort.

Her prayer routine became one of silent, open-hearted, grief-stricken communion with the Father, who she knew had not abandoned her.

After some months, the time came when she was emotionally strong enough to resume verbal communication with God. But the pain-forged intimacy they cultivated during those most difficult months will be hers for life.

Rebecca's faith survived—and, in fact, deepened—

because she held on to her true identity. Yet countless fellow believers actively deny their identity as God's children, thereby cutting themselves off from the privilege and power that goes with it. Why? For some, the history of a painful childhood may have left them with a warped father image that they project onto God. For others, the motive might be prideful independence. And still others, in their self-castigation, have convinced themselves that they are doing God a favor by staying away from Him.

What can liberate a person from these systems of denial? The answer is not *what*, but *Who*. Only God can break through the defenses we raise to ward off the weighty privilege of sonship or daughterhood.

EMOTIONAL HONESTY

King David, a man of great passions, took enormous risks with God. His prayers often had a raw edge to them—which may be why so many believers down through the millennia have found them so engaging and true to life. Confident of God's love, David did not restrain himself from honest expressions of bewilderment, pain, and even despair. Take Psalm 22:1–2, for example:

> My God, my God, why have you forsaken me?
>   Why are you so far from saving me,

> so far from the words of my groaning?
> O my God, I cry out by day, but you do not
> answer,
>   by night, and am not silent.

Was David in danger of going too far in his prayers—accusing God of inaction and indifference? No, David knew his standing with heaven. He knew he could pour out the contents of his troubled soul before the Lord, trusting Him to sort it all out. God was big enough to handle David's doubts and fears and longings. And as David opened his heart to the Lord, God would replace the erratic perceptions and emotional statements with eternal truths.

We see the outcome of David's forthrightness throughout the Psalms as, time after time, God brought him back around to an accurate expression of faith.

It was the same for Asaph, another prominent author of the Psalms. Take Psalm 73. After voicing his tortured doubts about God's justice in the world, in the end the psalmist acknowledges:

> When my heart was grieved
>   and my spirit embittered,
> I was senseless and ignorant;
>   I was a brute beast before you.
> Yet I am always with you;
>   you hold me by my right hand.

You guide me with your counsel,
>   and afterward you will take me into glory.
Whom have I in heaven but you?
>   And earth has nothing I desire besides you.
My flesh and my heart may fail,
>   but God is the strength of my heart
>   and my portion forever.

vv. 21–26

Notice that the psalm, which had started with faulty thinking, ended with both accuracy and intimacy.

God will never reject His children. Keeping this truth firmly in our grasp, we are free to be totally honest in His presence, not having to sugarcoat our feelings. (He knows all about them anyway!) When we do this, we are implicitly calling out to Him to rescue us from ourselves…to help us experience the freedom that belongs to His sons and daughters.

FREEDOM THROUGH THE SPIRIT

Sharon needed to experience God as Father. For twenty years she lived under the oppressive legalism of her husband, Greg. He blamed all their problems on her, and she believed him.

Mistrustful of her own judgment and afraid to make

decisions, she would take every slightest problem to Greg. But his silent condemnation left her feeling worse than ever. She sank into a deep depression.

At the same time, however, Sharon was growing—very gradually—in prayer. She didn't have any idea what words to use with God, so when she came across Psalm 73 (quoted above), she wrote out the last several verses and used them as her prayer guide throughout the day. "Lord, You're always with me. You'll hold my hand." And, "Lord, remember, You're the strength of my heart and my portion forever."

One day Greg found her staring at him strangely. He asked why she was looking at him that way, and she replied, "For the first time in our married life, I realize I'm a distinct person from you. I always thought I was just an extension of you." She was growing.

But Sharon's world crumbled around her when she discovered that Greg had been having an affair. He divorced Sharon and left her with their two children. She felt paralyzed and inadequate to face life alone. She wouldn't have known how to think about herself if not for the Scriptures to which she clung. More fervently than ever, she prayed their truth to God, and He faithfully helped her to recognize the unique and valuable person He had created her to be.

Slowly He gave her the confidence, with support from Christian brothers and sisters, to rebuild a new life. She courageously learned to handle her own finances, and she took initiative to acquire the skills necessary to hold a clerical job. Now Sharon ministers quietly but confidently to other women who are discovering intimacy and acceptance with God as their Father.

Sharon had allowed God's Holy Spirit to act as her freedom-agent, her liberator through the experience of relational prayer. Paul wrote, "Because you are sons [and daughters], God sent the Spirit of his Son into our hearts, the Spirit who calls out, 'Abba, Father.' So you are no longer a slave, but a son" (Galatians 4:6–7). When we pray, the Father hears the voice of His Son because the Spirit of Jesus lives in the believer.

And we don't need to worry when words fail us, because "the Spirit himself intercedes for us with groans that words cannot express. And…the Spirit intercedes for the saints in accordance with God's will" (Romans 8:26–27).

LIVING OUR IDENTITY

As we grow into our identity as God's son or daughter, we cultivate a new lifestyle. We start to think and act like our Father. We become "imitators of God…as dearly loved children" (Ephesians 5:1). Since we are already "light in the Lord," we now have the Spirit-empowered ability to "live as children of light" (v. 8).

During the early days of my growing faith, it was the new awareness that I was God's son and that He *liked* the idea of being my Father that encouraged me most. I was amazed that He enjoyed my company. Obstacles still sometimes interfere with our relationship, but I'm learning to present them to Him, to let *Him* remove them. There are times when I hide, but He always welcomes me back. I'm only beginning to grasp His love, which surpasses knowledge (Ephesians 3:17–19).

I can assure you, you don't need to hide from your Father.

PRAYER PRINCIPLE #5:

Prayer frees us from self-deception and reminds us that we're God's children.

Chapter Six

FREE TO HEAR
THE TRUTH

PRAYER AND THE WORLD'S LIES

But you, O Lord, said,
"Be clever as serpents and innocent as doves."
Let me retain innocence and simplicity
in the midst of this complex world.
I realize that I have to be informed,
that I have to study the many aspects of the problems
facing the world, and that I have to try to understand as well
as possible the dynamics of our contemporary society.
But what really counts is that all this information, knowledge,
and insight allows me to speak more clearly and unambiguously
your truthful word. Do not allow evil powers to seduce me
with the complexities of the world's problems,
but give me the strength to think clearly, speak freely,
and act boldly in your service. Give me the courage to show the
dove in a world so full of serpents.

HENRI NOUWEN (1932–1996), *A Cry for Mercy*[2]

The world is a supremely distracting and deceptive place. If you're like me, you have occasionally read a statement in the Bible and then thought, *That can't be right,* and tried to explain it away in light of the world's wisdom.

In God's presence, however, the truth makes more sense, and the world's lies make less. And even if the truth doesn't make sense, prayer fortifies our trust in the God who says it's true.

At a key turning point in history, God responded to prayer by opening His true Word to a misguided Augustinian monk. Throughout the early 1500s, Martin Luther fervently sought to be justified (made righteous before God) by the means that the church then taught—through virtuous acts, acceptance of church dogma, and participation in church ritual, including prayer. Luther devoted himself painstakingly to these disciplines.

When he was assigned to the chair of biblical studies at Wittenberg University, Scripture study became Luther's job as well as his passion. In 1515, he came upon Romans 1:17: "For in the gospel a righteousness from God is revealed, a righteousness that is by faith from first to last, just as it is written: 'The righteous will live by faith.'" Something about the passage intrigued Luther, but he couldn't pinpoint the issue. He pondered and prayed day and night, for many days.

Then suddenly it all made sense. Luther recalled, "I

grasped that the justice of God is that righteousness by which, through grace and sheer mercy, God justifies us through faith. Thereupon I felt myself to be reborn and to have gone through open doors into paradise."[3] The pieces fell into place. He realized that a person can be saved only through faith in the sacrifice of Jesus. He was freed from believing the lie that he could earn his own salvation.

Two years later Luther posted his ninety-five theses, which confronted the unscriptural errors then taught by the church, and the Protestant Reformation was launched.

Nearly five centuries later, another seeker wrestled in mental anguish. Amanda was a new Christian. She had been so badly hurt by her unstable mother and by past boyfriends that she believed her only means of emotional survival was to refuse to trust anyone. She also felt irresistibly drawn to sexually explicit entertainment and inappropriate relationships with men. Yet, at the same time, she wanted to become a woman of God, like other Christian women she knew.

She tried for over a year to conquer her sin habits, but each attempt ended in frustration. In her own eyes, she felt like scum.

In desperation, recognizing that she couldn't win the internal battle on her own, Amanda cried out to God, *Remake my mind. Come in and change my life!* In answer, He brought to her attention Philippians 4:8: "Finally, brothers, whatever is true, whatever is noble, whatever is right, whatever is pure, whatever is lovely, whatever is admirable—if anything is excellent or praiseworthy—think about such things."

This may not seem like a startling revelation, but that's exactly what it was for Amanda. Now she had a target to aim for. She prayed specifically for each of these qualities to become part of her thinking. She had found her life verse.

In time, she let down her defensive barriers and learned to trust the God who was extending Himself to her. He stirred within her a love for His true, unchanging Word and an undying gratitude for His faithfulness to her. He used His Word, other believers, and the ministry of His Holy Spirit to take away her affection for the addicting attractions of the world, and He replaced it with passion for Himself. She finally felt clean, whole, and acceptable.

FOR EVERY LIE, AN ANSWER

Even though everyone in our society has access to the Bible, none of us can understand God's truth without the illuminating ministry of God's Spirit (see John 16:13–14). During 1978, when I first read through Scripture and began to participate in Bible studies, I learned that praying over an open Bible invited the Spirit to unlock His truth and to free my mind to hear the Master's voice. By this means, He began using His Word to replace the world's lies with His truth. I found it encouraging that for every lie, Scripture had an answer.

Take, for example, the lie that freedom and fulfillment are to be found in material wealth. John D. Rockefeller said, "I have made many millions, but they have brought me no happiness." He discovered through hard experience the truth that, for centuries, God has offered in His Word: "Do not store up for yourselves treasures on earth.... But store up for yourselves treasures in heaven.... For where your treasure is, there your heart will be also" (Matthew 6:19–21).

For those who are deceived by the lure of power, God says, "Whoever wants to become great among you must be your servant, and whoever wants to be first must be your slave" (Matthew 20:26–27). For those who seek ultimate fulfillment through sensual pleasure, Scripture warns that such pursuits "lead straight to the grave" (Proverbs 5:5).

Pick a lie...any lie. God's Word gives a corresponding truth, opening the way to freedom. But we can only fully understand and obey God's truth when we walk daily in His presence.

ACTIVELY LISTENING TO GOD

God's Word and prayer complement each other as components of a two-way conversation. We show respect for

Scripture when we talk to God about what He's saying to us—praying back His Word to Him. The prayer-opened Word can guide us into even more effective prayer.

We also honor God's truth when we live by it. And this is to our advantage, because God's Word is "the perfect law that gives freedom" (James 1:25). Through prayer, God enhances our attentiveness to His truth—we take it more seriously—and He helps us understand the variety of ways He wants us to apply it. What is more, it is only in an attitude of prayerful humility and dependence that we demonstrate trust in God's Spirit, who empowers us to obey what we've read.

The psalmist understood that freedom comes through Spirit-led application of God's Word: "I run in the path of your commands, for you have set my heart free" (Psalm 119:32). Picture the freedom of *running* through life along the path of God's reality. How does this compare with your typical daily experience?

THE VOICE OF GOD?

Christians today debate heatedly about whether God speaks directly to the believer's mind and heart apart from His written Word. No one can argue that God isn't *able* to communicate this way—He can do anything He wants (Luke 1:37). The question is whether He *does* use this method for guiding us. I believe He does.

I know that this idea has been terribly abused. By opening this door, we make it possible for anyone to say anything and label it "God's Word." But there are a few guardrails along this road that can protect us from getting off onto the shoulder of falsehood. First of all, any real guidance from God would not contradict His written Word. Also, the fruit borne out of a person's life will demonstrate how closely attuned his heart is with God's (Matthew 7:15–20); we can discern from his conduct how reliable his "message from God" is.

The reason I believe God sometimes speaks directly to our hearts is that I've heard so many stories from people I trust attesting to God's guidance through inner prompting. That's why in my first novel, *Mission Compromised,* I wrote about an Arabic Christian named Eli Yusef Habib—a man devoted to prayer and humble submission to God. In the story, God guides Habib to the precise location in Iraq where he is able to rescue the book's main character, Peter Newman, and to manifest through his faith that there truly is a God who loves and cares for Newman. Habib is a fictional character, but his close relationship with God is based on true experience in my life and in the lives of other Christians.

All of this to say that, while God's written Word is certainly the primary source of His truth to us, as we devote our hearts to prayerful communion with Him, we become more pure and available vessels that He can direct by any means He chooses.

FREE TO HEAR HIM

Jesus promised that the truth would set us free (John 8:32). He assured us that His sheep will hear and know His voice (10:4, 16). How open are your ears to His truth? How open is your heart? However you answer these questions at this point in your life, God invites you to come closer to Him. As you do, His Word will cut through the fog of lies in the world. Talk with Him, and He will free you to hear and to heed His truth.

PRAYER PRINCIPLE #6:

*Prayer frees us to hear and heed God's truth,
not the world's lies.*

Chapter Seven

FREE FROM
MY "BEST"

Prayer and God's Unlimited Blessing

How did I come to submit my neck to your easy yoke,
and allow my shoulders to carry your light burden?
Instantly your yoke and burden, dear Christ,
felt wonderfully sweet, so much sweeter than
those vain delights which I had forsaken.
Indeed it was a joy to me to be deprived
of those joys which earlier I had feared to lose.
For you, O Lord, cast them away from me,
and in their place you yourself entered me,
bringing joy which is sweeter than any earthly pleasure.

Augustine of Hippo (354–430)

Having lived for three quarters of a century, Abram was comfortable and well established in the thriving Mesopotamian city of Ur. He was near his family and

everything he had ever known. His one significant disap-
pointment was his and Sarai's childlessness—a great dis-
grace in that culture. But he was doing his best.

Then God stepped in.

"Leave your country, your people and your father's
household and go to the land I will show you," God commanded (Genesis 12:1). Along with the command came
God's promise of numerous descendants and great blessing
through Abram on all nations of the world.

Bewildered but intrigued, Abram obeyed God and left
his home. Throughout the rest of his life, as an alien wan-
dering the land promised to him, he would take possession
of only one small plot to use as a burial site for his wife.

Some years after he had arrived in God's Promised
Land, Abram and Sarai were still unable to conceive. So
Sarai, with Abram's consent, decided it was in their best
interest to produce this promised offspring their own way.
Abram slept with Sarai's servant Hagar, and she bore his
first son, Ishmael, who became the ancestor of all the Arab
nations.

But what Abram thought was best—to produce his
own heir—fell far short of God's dream. One day God
appeared to Abram and confirmed that His promise would
be fulfilled through a son born to Sarai. To highlight this
historic turning point, God changed their names to
Abraham and Sarah. True to God's promise, Isaac was born

one year later, to Abraham, age one hundred, and Sarah, ninety-one.

But God was not finished fulfilling His promises. We can now look back and see that it was through Abraham's son Isaac that God produced His chosen people, Israel. And it was through Israel that God brought His Son, Jesus the Messiah, into the world to live and to die on our behalf. Not only did Abraham become the physical father of all Israel, but he also became the spiritual father of all who would trust Christ with the same faith Abraham expressed toward God (Romans 4:16–17).

This nomadic patriarch, who would otherwise have disappeared into obscurity, became known as "God's friend" (James 2:23). Because Abraham desired above all else to walk closely with God, God responded by doing far more than Abraham could have dreamed. He used this man as His instrument for carrying out His world-wide, millennia-spanning plan for the salvation of billions and for the establishment of His kingdom on earth.

OUR BEST VERSUS GOD'S BEST

We humans are limited beings. That's not a bad thing. It's a simple fact of God's wise design. We don't know everything, so we need His guidance. We can't do everything, so we need His power. We can't love perfectly, so we need His heart.

During my younger years I failed to grasp how limited my vision was. To me, "the best" meant becoming the bravest marine and the sharpest officer the Corps had ever seen. And doing it on my own. My best was to save South Vietnam—to lead the men who would preserve freedom in yet another region of the globe.

These were good desires, but in my myopia, I was cutting myself off from the much greater good God wanted to lavish on me. I didn't have to stop being a marine or stop contributing to freedom in the world, but God had another mission at home that only I could carry out. There was a woman He commanded me to love and care for, and there were growing children who needed their father's time. I thank God that He broadened my perspective to see the bigger picture. If I had neglected my family, little else I would have done in my life would have amounted to much in heaven's ledgers.

God is the one who "is able to do immeasurably more than all we ask or imagine, according to his power that is at work within us" (Ephesians 3:20).

It's as though we live in the bottom of a ditch. As long as we stay there, our horizons are radically constricted. If we don't know any better, we naturally think the inside of the ditch is all there is to our world...the best there is.

When I pray, God responds by lifting me up, allowing me to see beyond my constricted horizons into the infinitely wide vistas of His reality. Prayer opens the way for God to work out *His* dream for my life, to provide *His* resources for my fulfillment, to pour *His* unlimited blessings into my life and heart.

God can even teach us this lesson through our kids' toys. Syd's son Nathan has been a Legomaniac all his life—he still is today, as a married adult. One Christmas Nathan wanted a particular Lego set that contained some specialized pieces. Now, you have to understand that Nathan's wasn't just an if-you-get-around-to-it kind of request. It was one of those drop-a-hint-every-day-since-Thanksgiving requests.

But Syd didn't give Nathan what he asked for.

Syd did his homework and discovered a different set containing the same special pieces, but three times as large. He bought it and wrapped it for the big day. Though Nathan was adamant about the "best" gift Syd could give him, to Nathan's delight Syd surpassed it on Christmas morning.

To this day, when Syd is conscious that God might have far more to give than Syd's imagination allows him to ask, he says, "God, this is a Lego prayer. Please answer according to the abundance of Your riches." Here is a man who knows what he doesn't know.

PRAYING FOR GOD'S BEST

So what is God's best for each of us? That varies from person to person. Talk to God, and, in His time, He will help you discover His perfect plan for your life.

I do, however, know a few principles that might help you recognize and seek His best when you see it.

First, *God's best always begins and ends with Himself.* This is the discovery Augustine voiced in the prayer quoted at the beginning of this chapter. And we've already heard the psalmist's heart: "Whom have I in heaven but you? And earth has nothing I desire besides you" (Psalm 73:25). Finding and knowing God is what prayer is all about.

Second, *God's best always involves our obedience.* Notice, for example, that Jesus' promise of abundant blessing begins with a command: "Give, and it will be given to you. A good measure, pressed down, shaken together and running over, will be poured into your lap" (Luke 6:38). As you pray for God's best, offer yourself as His servant.

Third, *God gives His best to those who ask for it—and ask with pure motives.* "You do not have, because you do not ask God. When you ask, you do not receive, because you ask with wrong motives, that you may spend what you get on your pleasures" (James 4:2–3). God is so gracious that He gives blessing even to those who don't ask. But He reserves His best for those who do.

And fourth, *God's best is not always pain free.* In fact,

sometimes God's best comes *through* pain. Peter explained that God allows suffering and hardship "so that your faith—of greater worth than gold, which perishes even though refined by fire—may be proved genuine and may result in praise, glory and honor when Jesus Christ is revealed" (1 Peter 1:7). Even Jesus, who never sinned, "learned obedience from what he suffered," and thereby became perfectly prepared to do His saving work (Hebrews 5:8; see also 2:10; 5:7–9).

When we pray about our pain—whether it's ahead of us, behind us, or right on top of us—God may not show us His reasons, but He assures us that He is in control and that He has a wise and loving purpose for everything. This kind of insight sustained my family and me through five long and difficult years of congressional hearings and criminal trials. During that time I was often reminded of a picture in my marine friend's office. It shows a raft riding through rough rapids, and the caption reads: "God doesn't promise you a smooth passage—just a safe delivery."

WHEN PAIN IS BEST

Pain was instrumental in the life of the seventeenth-century mathematician and philosopher Blaise Pascal. Pascal lived only thirty-nine years, but in this short time he left an intellectual and spiritual legacy that has impacted the entire

Western world. He was plagued by debilitating illness from age twenty-four on, and during one particularly difficult period near the end of his life he wrote a prayer "On the Good Use of Sickness." The prayer, which in at least one English edition fills seven pages, begins:

> O Lord, whose Spirit is so good and gracious in all things, and who is so merciful that not only prosperities but even the adversities that happen to your elect are the effects of your mercy, give me grace not to act like the unbelievers in the state you bring me into by your justice. Instead, like a true Christian, help me to acknowledge you as my Father and my God, in whatever circumstances you may place me. For no change of my circumstances can ever alter your will for my life. You are ever the same, though I may be subject to change. You are no less God when you are afflicting and punishing me than when you are consoling and showing compassion.[4]

Pascal understood that God's best was far beyond anything he could imagine and that God's method for fulfilling His good purpose in Pascal's life was not subject to Pascal's approval. He was willing to allow pain to do its work in his life because he knew God as his Father.

Pascal's attitude reflects that of the apostle John: "How

great is the love the Father has lavished on us, that we should be called children of God! And that is what we are!" (1 John 3:1). When we draw close to God, we enjoy fresh amazement at the privilege of being His children, and we become better prepared to receive all the best He offers His kids. There's no way you can foresee the unlimited blessing your Father has in store for you. Pray, and you'll find it.

PRAYER PRINCIPLE #7:

Prayer frees us from our limited perspective so that we can receive God's unlimited blessing.

Chapter Eight

FREE TO SERVE OTHERS

PRAYER AND MY PRIDE

*O you who are good and do good, who extend your
loving-kindness to all mankind, the work of your hands,
your image, capable of knowing and loving you eternally:
suffer me to exclude none, O Lord, from my charity,
who are the objects of your mercy; but let me treat all
my neighbors with that tender love which is due to
your servants and to your children.
Let your love to me, O blessed Savior,
be the pattern of my love to them.*

CHARLES WESLEY (1707–1788)

With a bit of imagination, we can step into the pages of
Scripture and enter a certain room—at a moment when the
discomfort level was pushing into the red zone. Since the
group was meeting in secret, no servants were available to

perform the usual before-meal foot washing. This kind of situation was not uncommon. In the absence of a servant, the person who was of lowest social status was expected to wash the feet of the rest.

But there was the rub. Who was the lowliest of the Twelve? Was it Matthew, who had served for years as a despised tax collector? Was it Simon Peter, the uneducated fisherman? Or maybe Simon the Zealot, who had once participated in illegal political action against Rome? No one volunteered.

Outside the twilight grew darker, and inside the men exchanged nervous banter.

The meal was served, and still their feet were coated with the dust of the day's travels. They waited for thanks to be offered before eating. But nothing happened. A few men shot accusing looks at each other.

Only the One sitting in the place of honor seemed to be resting at ease. For another few seconds He watched His disciples squirm. Then, without a word, the Teacher stood from His place, stripped down like a servant, and wrapped a towel around His waist.

He picked up the bowl of water their host had provided and moved to the first disciple, washing his feet in the water then drying them with the towel with which He was girded.

Every pair of eyes stared aghast. Several of the men

were now wishing that they had broken down and done the task themselves. The Teacher's humiliation was the height of embarrassment.

Jesus progressed from one to the next, around the room, delayed only by a brief argument with Simon Peter. Then He washed His own feet, donned His clothes, and sat back in His place. The meal sat untouched.

The Teacher gathered His thoughts and asked, "Do you understand what I have done for you?"

A couple shook their heads. Most were afraid to respond.

"You call me 'Teacher' and 'Lord,'" Jesus continued, "and rightly so, for that is what I am. Now that I, your Lord and Teacher, have washed your feet, you also should wash one another's feet."

The Teacher spoke on, and the men gradually regained the courage to eat. It was only the beginning of a long, confusing night.

THE BARRIER OF PRIDE

What was it that enabled Jesus, the Master, to serve His men in a manner that befitted a slave? Early in the passage from which this story is taken (John 13:1–17), John gives us the answer: "Jesus knew that the Father had put all things under his power, and that he had come from God and was returning to God; so he got up from the meal," and He washed His disciples' feet (vv. 3–4). Humility came easily to Jesus because He had no doubt about who He was.

The freedom to serve others begins with a changed attitude toward ourselves—with the recognition of our identity and relationship with God. It is the one who has a false view of himself who cannot help but try to prove himself, often by walking over others. Insecurity and pride are two sides of the same coin.

How do we gain a healthy self-awareness? As we saw in chapter 5, we discover who we truly are through prayer and God's Word. The Christian's healthy self-image is learned—and learned most effectively in the presence of our Father.

According to Martin Luther, "A Christian is a perfectly free lord of all, subject to none. A Christian is a perfectly dutiful servant of all, subject to all." When we pray for ourselves and those around us, God responds by changing our hearts, assuring us of our royal status as His children, removing pride and selfishness, and freeing us to serve others with a sense of personal security.

THE BARRIER OF BITTERNESS

Bitterness is another barrier holding us back from serving people. We are quick to quote Jesus' commands to "love your enemies" and to "do good to those who hate you"

(Luke 6:27), but living them out is not quite so easy. If we refuse to forgive those who have wronged us, we are not free to serve them in the spirit of Jesus' example or teaching.

Only by drawing upon God's presence, power, and truth can we experience inward change and begin to express true outward forgiveness and love.

Ernest Gordon, in his book *To End All Wars,* tells of his capture by the Japanese early in World War II. He and tens of thousands of other Allied POWs endured three and a half years in a series of prison camps in Malaya and Thailand, along the valley of the famed River Kwai. These POWs comprised the initial work force that was compelled to build the Burma railroad, intended for the invasion of India. The project was initially supposed to require six years, but the prisoners were forced to finish it in one.

Gordon writes, "During the four years of their ascendancy the Japanese military violated every civilized code. They murdered prisoners overtly by bayoneting, shooting, drowning, beating or decapitation; they murdered them covertly by working them beyond the limit of human endurance, starving them, torturing them and denying them medical care."[5] Special methods of torture were reserved for those who failed to comply with orders.

The prisoners were allowed to start a church. Through the teaching of such Bible stories as the Good Samaritan and Jesus' forgiveness toward His murderers, many of the

men found themselves wrestling with the challenge to forgive their Japanese captors. When they routinely recited the
Lord's Prayer, they stumbled over "and forgive us our tres-
passes as we forgive those that trespass against us." But
some prayed it in earnest.

And God answered.

Gordon describes many of the prisoners' sacrificial acts
of kindness—toward each other and also toward their enemies. One day late in the war, the prisoners crossed paths
with several railcars full of wounded Japanese on their way
back from the Burmese front. No longer fit for action, these
soldiers had been discarded by the Japanese army and left to
their own devices to return several hundred miles to
Bangkok, where presumably they would receive medical aid.
Many had died on the way, and more were at death's door.
Their open wounds were putrid and crawling with maggots.

At a stopping point along the track, the Allied prisoners and the Japanese wounded found themselves resting
directly across from each other, both groups emaciated
physically and emotionally. Without a word, most of the
officers from Gordon's section of prisoners took from their
own meager supply of food, water, and rags and, ignoring
the prohibitions of their Japanese guards, ministered to the
needs of their enemy.

No one has ever experienced freedom greater than
those prisoners did that day.[6]

PRAYER IS SERVICE

We pray in order to cultivate hearts that serve. But we must also recognize that prayer itself is effective ministry—more effective than anything else we do. We are never powerless to help others who are in need—physical hardship, emotional distress, spiritual attack…anything. We can pray.

At age nineteen, Shirley became pregnant by her boyfriend and gave up her son for adoption. Some years later she became strong in her Christian faith. Though she had no idea where her son was or even what his name was, she began to contend habitually for him in prayer, sometimes all night long, praying various Scriptures on his behalf. In April 1973, God brought her to Jeremiah 31:16–17: "Restrain your voice from weeping and your eyes from tears, for your work will be rewarded…. There is hope for your future…. Your children will return to their own land." As she had done with many other passages, she labeled this one with the date and "My son."

Many years later, Shirley decided she wanted to find her son and, if possible, to cultivate a relationship with him. She hired private investigators, and in time they discovered his identity and location. His name was John, and he was the pastor of a small church.

Shirley and her husband traveled twelve hundred miles to meet John. His church was renting a meeting room in a hotel for their services, so Shirley and her husband checked into a room in the same hotel. When Shirley went down to attend John's service, she saw him huddled with his ministry team, their heads bowed.

The first time Shirley saw her adult son, he was praying.

Shirley's revelation of her identity to John is a story of its own. It was, to say the least, revolutionary for them both. Some time later it occurred to John to ask her if he could peruse her Bible and her notes in it. He was looking for a particular date.

There it was, right beside Jeremiah 31:16–17: April 1973, the very month in which John had placed his faith in Christ.

Galatians 5:13 tells us to use our freedom to "serve one another in love." Shirley expressed her freedom in Christ and served her son faithfully through prayer all those years. Her ministry of prayer may have made a greater difference in John's life than if she had been with him in person.

Whom will you serve?

PRAYER PRINCIPLE #8:

Prayer frees us from pride and bitterness,
enabling us to serve others.

Chapter Nine

FREE TO SERVE GOD

PRAYER AND MY PURPOSE

*Lord, accept me; I here present myself,
praying to live only in thee and to thee.
Let me be as the bullock which stands between the plough
and the altar, to work or to be sacrificed;
and let my motto be, "Ready for either."*
CHARLES HADDON SPURGEON (1834–1892)

All Dee Duke wanted to do was to run a dairy farm. He had attended Bible college in order to help as a lay minister in his rural church, but he much preferred the company of cows to people.

God had other plans. In 1976, Dee was invited to serve as senior pastor of Jefferson Baptist Church in the small town of Jefferson, Oregon. For six months, Dee wrestled with God over the decision, and God won. Dee took the position.

Thirteen years later, Dee was preparing to quit. It had all been a mistake. He didn't know how to love his people, and they didn't trust him. There was continual division and bickering within the church. He considered himself a failure.

About this same time Dee received an invitation to attend a four-day pastors' prayer summit on the Oregon coast. He discarded the invitation, but then received another explaining that a generous donor would pay for him to attend. *Maybe this is good timing,* he thought. *I can skip the prayer sessions, go for some walks on the beach, and write my letter of resignation.*

But again God had a different purpose in mind. At the prayer summit, Dee experienced a personal revolution. He returned to Jefferson with a written list of specific goals for his growth in prayer. He read the list every day and began to devote hours at a time to prayer.

It has been fifteen years since that turning point. Dee now spends at least three cumulative hours each day in conversation with God. He's still the pastor of Jefferson Baptist Church, which draws eleven hundred people each Sunday in a town of eighteen hundred. Because of his example and his persistent teaching on prayer, his people also know how to pray faithfully. The church has become unified and vibrant, and the people trust and love Dee.

In any given year, Dee mentors five groups of a dozen

pastors, meeting with each group several times a year and supporting each pastor by means of individual e-mail accountability. He speaks around the country and has started and sustains church plants in Africa and Asia. The impact of one praying dairyman is now being felt around the world.[7]

One of Dee's favorite Scripture passages is John 14:12–14, where Jesus, on the night before He was crucified, began with: "I tell you the truth, anyone who has faith in me will do what I have been doing. He will do even greater things than these, because I am going to the Father" (v. 12).

But that is only the first verse of the passage, which is often quoted in isolation, leading to the mistaken perception that we might do our "greater things" by ourselves. Jesus immediately continued, "And I will do whatever you ask in my name, so that the Son may bring glory to the Father. You may ask me for anything in my name, and I will do it" (vv. 13–14). Just as it was Jesus performing miracles during His earthly life, so now it's Jesus who continues to do great works through us…in response to our prayers.

FREE TO SERVE

The nineteenth-century preacher Phillips Brooks said, "No man in this world attains to freedom from any slavery except by entrance into some higher servitude. There is no such thing as an entirely free man conceivable."

Jesus agreed. He taught that all men and women were designed to serve—the question left to us is which master we will choose (Matthew 6:24). Every Christian struggles with counterfeit masters that try to divert our loyalty. But at our root we all have a desire to serve God and to serve Him significantly, freed from hindrances and distractions in order to move forward with passion. True freedom is not absolute "independence," but rather a restful dependence in the purpose and plan of God.

How, then, can we gain freedom to serve our chosen Master in a way that makes an eternal difference? Through prayer.

As we abide in Christ (John 15:1–8), He strengthens our faithfulness to Him, and we find fulfillment in His service. Prayer draws us deeper into love and gratitude toward Him. Through the relationship of prayer, we gain clarification of our purpose in His kingdom work. And in God's presence we find the strength and vision to move ahead boldly.

The prospect of living a meaningless, purposeless existence is one of the most depressing and frightening destinies I can envision. Through prayer, God frees us for steadfast, forward-moving action that impacts eternity.

PRAY COURAGEOUSLY

Two weeks after John Grinalds prayed and God healed my back, our battalion stood in formation on the pier, waiting for Grinalds to give us the order to deploy to the Mediterranean. In front of two thousand men, the lieutenant colonel strode over to where I was standing at attention. Rather than giving the official order, as has been repeated according to tradition since 1775, John Grinalds reached into his map pocket, pulled out a Bible, and slapped it against my chest.

"Here, Major," he said. "Read this on your way across the Atlantic Ocean."

So I did. By the time we arrived in Spain, I'd made my way through the entire Old Testament and come to Matthew 8. In verses 5–13, I encountered a fellow warrior. A Roman centurion, in command of a hundred men, approached Jesus and asked Him to heal his paralyzed servant. And Jesus granted the soldier's request.

My point here is to highlight the courage the centurion displayed in simply approaching Jesus in the first place. Under Roman law, Jesus was a seditionist because He was teaching people to follow a King other than Caesar. If the centurion had been caught even talking to a seditionist, he would have been found guilty of sedition himself and sentenced to death. This man had risked not only his career, but also his life in order to ask for Jesus' help...for a servant.

John Grinalds displayed that same courage the day he prayed for my back and then again when he ordered me to read the Bible. It is contrary to the code of military justice in every branch of the service for an officer to proselytize a subordinate. On either of those occasions, one of the senior onlookers could have walked up and cited Grinalds for proselytizing, and it would have been the end of his career. But they had all come to respect the courage he displayed through his actions.

It's with this courage, and the confidence that God will answer our prayers, that we must learn to pray. God doesn't always answer the way we expect Him to, but we can live with absolute certainty that He hears and that He always answers in keeping with His sovereign purpose.

DON'T GIVE UP

Jesus taught that we ought always to pray with persistence (Luke 11:5–10; 18:1–8). The best translation of Jesus' command, "Ask and it will be given to you; seek and you will find; knock and the door will be opened to you" (Luke 11:9), drawing out the text's original meaning, is: *"Keep on asking…keep on seeking…keep on knocking."*

God never tires of hearing the same request over and over, as long as we mean what we say. The English writer Thomas Fuller said: "A good prayer, though often used, is still fresh and fair in the eyes and ears of heaven."

Also, though we're often forgetful, the fact remains that we are engaged in a fierce battle on the spiritual plane. If we want to gain victory, prayer is our main weapon, and we must wield it with purpose and tenacity (Ephesians 6:18).

One of the notable outbreaks of the spiritual battle into our physical world was the Thirty Years' War, which took place between 1718 and 1748. When Count Nikolaus von Zinzendorf saw that Christians in Moravia and Bohemia were being persecuted, he felt great compassion for them. In 1722, he provided refuge on his property in Germany for several hundred exiles, and they established the community called Herrnhut ("Under the Lord's Watch").

Five years later, a group of twenty-four men and twenty-four women from this community began a round-the-clock prayer meeting. More joined them to ensure that every minute of every day was covered with prayer. This became known as the prayer meeting that lasted one hundred years. Within months, as God provided these Christians with fresh vision, the group began sending missionaries to the West Indies, Greenland, Turkey, and Lapland.

Many of the missionaries died or were imprisoned, but the group's spiritual momentum was such that more ventured out to take their places. Within a decade, this community of six hundred had sent out seventy missionaries.

Before William Carey, the "Father of Modern Missions," made his impact, over three hundred Moravian missionaries had already launched out with the gospel.

The shock wave from their prayers continued to spread through history. It was the fervor of the Moravian missions movement that sparked the conversions of John and Charles Wesley, leaders of the Great Awakening that swept across Europe and America.[8]

God's purpose for you may not be to ignite a worldwide missions movement. It may instead be to care well for your family, to share Christ's love and truth with a neighbor, or to sweep the floors of a homeless shelter. Whatever God's dream for your life—large and spectacular, or "small" and quiet—you can be assured that He will work through you to impact eternity. But you will only find His dream and the fulfillment that comes from living it out in His presence, seeking His heart.

PRAYER PRINCIPLE #9:

Prayer frees us to know and fulfill God's great purpose for our lives.

Chapter Ten

LIBERATED
FOR LIFE

My God and my All!
What greater blessing can I receive than your love?
What greater wealth can I possess than your grace?
What greater pleasure can I enjoy than your presence?
THOMAS À KEMPIS (C. 1380–1471)

Kay felt completely alone. She stood on the dirt path, look-ing up at her house. A house that now seemed half empty. How could she ever learn to live in a world where she was a widow?

She longed for her husband's embrace, but in that moment she recalled another comforting embrace. She remembered how, when she was a girl, her father so often picked her up and hugged her—when she was hurt, when she was scared, when she was disappointed.

Then, in her mind's eye, Kay pictured another little girl, crying because she had skinned her knee. The girl ran through an immense, fabulously ornate mansion—greater and more spectacular than anything built on earth. At the end of a long corridor stood a huge, sparkling gold door, which was closed. On either side stood two magnificently dressed guards holding huge spears and blocking the entrance.

But the little girl ran boldly to the door, crying, "Abba!" The guards flung open the doors and heralded her arrival: "The daughter of the King! The daughter of the King!" Court was in session, and the greatest and most powerful beings in all the universe surrounded the King. But the girl paid them no heed, running straight through their midst, up the steps to the throne. She leaped into the King's arms. She was home.

The King reached up and gently wiped away her tears. He smoothed her hair and tenderly held her injured leg. Then He said, "Now, tell your Father all about it."

Kay's mind returned to the dirt path and the half-empty house. She continued into the house, through to the bedroom, where she knelt and talked to her Father.[9]

YOUR FATHER'S HEART

This experience from Kay Arthur, a popular author and Bible teacher, illustrates the depth of relationship I also discovered when I came to understand who God really is. Throughout this book, I've tried to share a number of ways in which prayer—not just prayer as a thing we do or words we say, but prayer as an intimate relationship—brings freedom to the believer's life.

If you have trusted Jesus Christ as your Savior, take a few minutes and consider how each of the principles we've examined brings to light the heart of the Father who loves you as His son or daughter.

Prayer Principle #1: Prayer liberates us to live as we were designed, in intimate relationship with God.
God's greatest desire for you is freedom—freedom to live a holy, fruitful life. Will you let down your defenses and allow Him to show you that you can trust Him?

Prayer Principle #2: Prayer brings continually renewed freedom from guilt.
God is more eager to forgive than you may be to receive forgiveness. Will you hand over to Him the burden of your past?

Prayer Principle #3: Prayer frees us from the stranglehold of sin's power.
In God's presence, He fills you with righteousness and wisdom. Look inside and see how hungry you are for His character in your life.

Prayer Principle #4: Prayer frees us from anxiety as we come to know God's faithful heart.
God is powerful enough, wise enough, and caring enough to take care of you. Will you entrust Him with your fears about the future?

Prayer Principle #5: Prayer frees us from self-deception and reminds us that we're God's children.
Your Father chose you to be His child and is proud that you wear His name. Consider talking with Him about the thoughts that might make you doubt this.

Prayer Principle #6: Prayer frees us to hear and heed God's truth, not the world's lies.
In God's presence, truth comes clear, and God's truth is liberating. Will you seek His help that you might live in the world with wisdom and discernment?

Prayer Principle #7: Prayer frees us from our limited perspective so that we can receive God's unlimited blessing.
God has far greater plans for you than you can possibly imagine. Will you confess your limited horizons and invite Him to raise you up to receive all His possibilities?

Prayer Principle #8: Prayer frees us from pride and bitterness, enabling us to serve others.
Your Father's desire is that you would love others as He does. Why not invite Him to transform your heart to be like His?

Prayer Principle #9: Prayer frees us to know and fulfill God's great purpose for our lives.
God made you so that you would be most thoroughly fulfilled serving Him. Examine the sense of purpose and destiny He has planted deep inside you, and invite Him to fulfill His dream in your life.

THE DOORWAY TO FREEDOM

It's my prayer that the heart of God would become your greatest source of encouragement and refreshment for the rest of your life. I've given you some words on paper, but God offers Himself—every day, every moment.

In my early years, I thought I was as close to God as anyone could be. But, as I've shared already, I only knew *about* Him. I had not met Him in Person.

When I entered into the personal, liberating relationship with God that I now enjoy, the way I did it was simply to recognize that I had disobeyed God—I confessed that I was guilty and that I deserved an eternal death sentence. But I also knew that God had sent His Son, Jesus, to be declared "guilty" of my sin and to die in my place, and I accepted the gift of His sacrifice for me.

At that moment, God liberated me from the condemnation I deserved, and He adopted me as His son…forever.

If you haven't trusted Jesus as your Savior, all you need

to do is what I did. If these words reflect your true desire, you can say to Him, "Lord, I'm guilty, and I don't deserve You. But I do accept the gift of Your Son's death in my place. Thank You for forgiving me and for accepting me as Your child."

In that moment, you'll enter into a whole new universe of freedom.

If you have questions regarding a relationship with Jesus Christ, God wants you to have the answers.
You can talk to someone at the Billy Graham Evangelistic Association by calling toll-free
(from within the United States and Canada)
1-877-2GRAHAM (1-877-247-2426) or
by contacting them through their website at
www.billygraham.org/contactus.

We also encourage you to seek guidance from a Bible-teaching church near you. God's family is there to help.

The publisher and author would love to hear your comments about this book. *Please contact us at:*
www.bigchangemoments.com

NOTES

1. From interview and Shel Arensen, *Come Away: How to Have a Personal Prayer Retreat* (Grand Rapids, MI: Kregel, 2003), 171–2.

2. From *A Cry for Mercy* by Henri J. M. Nouwen, (c) 1981 by Henri J. M. Nouwen. Used by permission of Doubleday, a division of Random House, Inc.

3. Bruce L. Shelley, *Church History in Plain Language* (Nashville, TN: Thomas Nelson/Word, 1995), 239.

4. James M. Houston, ed., *The Mind on Fire: An Anthology of the Writings of Blaise Pascal* (Portland, OR: Multnomah, 1989), 285.

5. Ernest Gordon, *To End All Wars* (Grand Rapids, MI: Zondervan, 1963), 48.

6. Ibid., 48, 64–5, 154–6, 196–7.

7. Paraphrased from Dee Duke with Brian Smith, *The Time Is Now, Developing a Lifestyle of Prayer* (Portland, OR: Pray Afghanistan, 2002), 7–10. A few details were also taken from other selections.

8. From Robert J. Morgan, *Nelson's Complete Book of Stories, Illustrations, and Quotes* (Nashville, TN: Thomas Nelson, 2000), 625–6.

9. Paraphrased from Gloria Gaither, comp. and ed., *What My Parents Did Right* (Nashville, TN: Star Song Publishing Group, 1991), 16–8.

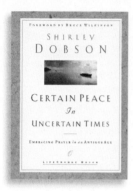
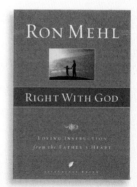

BIG CHANGE

SMALL BOOKS
BIG CHANGE